PIGGIE FINDS A Family

Piggie didn't remember much about his old life, but he remembered being alone a lot. When he was a puppy, there were a lot of people around, but lately it's just been him. When Piggie was a puppy, his ears used to be soft and floppy and hung down. Now they were small and pointy and stuck straight up. He missed his floppy ears.

One morning, Piggie felt hungry, and his tummy was grumbling.
Wasn't it breakfast time? He waited and waited, but no one came to feed him.
He wiggled out of his collar and squeezed through a hole in the fence.

On the other side there was a big road and lots of cars. The hot sidewalk hurt his paws. "Maybe I should find a place to rest," he thought.

After a while, a big car pulled up next to Piggie, shading him from the sun. A lady got out and put down food and water which he quickly drank and ate. He gave her a high five with his big paw to say thanks! She picked him up and put him in the car.

He didn't know where they were going but it was nice to lie down in the air conditioning. He closed his eyes for a nap.

The car stopped, and there was a building with dogs barking. The closer they got to the building, the louder the barks became. Piggie saw the words "Animal Shelter"... he tilted his head, "What is this place?"

Inside it was loud and crowded with a lot to smell and see. They walked down a hallway filled with all kinds of different dogs that seemed to be barking at him.

When they finally stopped, some new people sat down on a soft blanket with him. They said he was stinky, but they pet him anyway. "Everyone is being so nice to me!"

She told Piggie that they were going to try to figure out if he had a family. They used a big machine to scan for "chips" but didn't find any. He heard them say no one was going to pick him up. Piggie was confused, "If no one is coming, is this my new home forever?"

They put Piggie into a kennel. He watched as some of the other dogs went home with families. He overheard someone say they got "adopted", "Does that mean they get to go home with them?" He wasn't allowed inside at the old place. He wanted to be in someone's home too.

A lady came in the door and Piggie sat up. She said, "I'm looking for a dog to go for runs and on hikes with."

Adopt, Don't Shop

Say hello! I'm adoptable!

Piggie laid back down in his kennel. "Well, I can't run, and I definitely can't go on hikes with these paws."

Piggie watched as the kids ran over to the younger dogs.
"I'm not a puppy anymore. Will anybody want to take me home?"
He used his paws to smush his blankets into
a pile to rest his chin on. Piggie let out a big sigh,
"Ahhhhh, time for another nap."

Piggie woke up when he heard someone say "Awwwww!" He opened his eyes.
A couple opened the door to his kennel to meet him. He gave his head a big
shake to wake himself up.
"Time to be friendly and show them what a good boy I am!"
They brought him outside to get to know him better.

Outside, Piggie was on his best behavior. They gave him scratches behind his tiny ears. They laughed and said he was cute. Piggie put his paw up in case they wanted a high five. They did!

They sat together for a little while. Soon, they decided
that they wanted to take him home!
"I think I'm getting adopted too!"
He looked at the adoption papers. He couldn't believe it.
"Am I really getting adopted? Is this my new family?"

Piggie loved that they carried him everywhere. After all the excitement, he was too tired to walk to the car. When he was being carried, he felt like he was flying!

The whole car ride Piggie was thinking about what it will be like to have a family. He wondered if he would get to live inside with them.
"I wonder if they will play with me every day?" Piggie was so excited. He stuck his head out of the window and felt the wind on his tongue.

Once they got out, Piggie started sniffing around. His new family headed towards the front door. Piggie got worried for a minute, "Oh man, I'm so slow... don't leave me behind, guys!" He slowly made his way to the front of the house where they were waiting for him.

Inside the house, two cats stared at him. Piggie had never met a cat before, but he hoped they could be friends. He crouched down to see if the gray one wanted to play. He let out a playful bark, and the white fluffy one jumped up on the couch and arched her back, cautiously looking at Piggie.

At the old place, Piggie never got to go inside and didn't have any toys. He rolled over on his wrinkly back with a squeaky toy in his mouth, loving every second in his new home.

Piggie was so happy; he had so many toys it was hard to pick a favorite. He had a ramp to get up onto the couch on his own and lay in the sunbeams. Hanging with his new family while they watched TV was so relaxing.

Piggie was settling in and feeling at home, but one day, he felt really sick. His parents didn't know how to make him feel better. They called the vet, and she said Piggie needed to come into the hospital right away!

They got to the hospital and took Piggie inside to the front desk where they talked to his new family for a really long time.

The doctor took an Xray of his whole body. They said his heart was the reason he was feeling so sick.

Piggie was confused, "Something is wrong with my heart? Is that why I get tired so fast? Is that why I'm so bad at running, and why I pant all the time?"

The doctor said Piggie had to stay at the hospital for a few days. The doctor picked him up in her arms, and his new family waved goodbye.

The doctor said he needed three shots. Piggie gulped and his eyes went wide, "THREE?" She came over and gave him some snuggles. With warm hands, she gave him scratches behind the ears. Piggie tried not to be scared. He felt brave and closed his eyes in anticipation, "These will make me feel better!"

After a couple days, his family picked him up. Piggie was ready to go home and snuggle with them on the couch. He still felt a little bit crummy; all he could do was lie down and sleep. He wanted to let his family know he was okay, so every once in a while, he gave them kisses on the face and gentle high fives.

Piggie was finally feeling rested, and after a few days and lots of love and attention...he was finally better! They all went to the park and Piggie could walk faster, play longer, and breathe better. Piggie was so grateful and made sure to show it.

He loved being around people and soaked up every minute of fun and happiness. If this is what being adopted feels like, he wanted every single dog in the world to feel like this. Every dog should have a family.

"My name is Piggie, and lots of people love me. The staff at the animal shelter saw that I was special and helped me find a home. The people at the hospital made me healthy again. My new family gives me more love and attention than I ever knew was possible. They tell me that every day from now on is going to be my best day ever! I'm so excited for my new life, and I'm going to have so much fun. Now I know what love feels like."

Piggie was treated for heartworm disease which pets can get when they are bitten by infected mosquitoes. Heartworm is a parasite that causes problems in a pet's lungs, heart, and other organs. Pets do better if heartworm is detected early. Piggie was lucky to have a loving family that noticed signs of this disease and started treatment right away. Veterinarians recommend that all dogs get tested for heartworm once per year. While most dogs can be successfully treated for heartworm, prevention is preferred. This serious disease can be prevented with monthly pills, topical treatment, or injections. Be sure to speak with your veterinarian about heartworm prevention and treatment.

Microfilariae enter bloodstream

Mosquito bites infected animal, ingests microfilariae

Larvae migrate to the heart

Mosquito becomes infected

Infected mosquito bites an animal

Remember to mark the date so you don't forget your monthly preventatives!

August

You can use a dog safe bug spray on your pet when outside for extra protection

DOG SAFE

Special thanks to: Tunie & Dillon, Binks & Rush, Andrea, Banff & Jasper, Mike & Karen, Mom & Dad, Yeleny, Gale & Gene Cartledge, Marc, Lucy & Colene, Fran Boland & Rascal, the Caputo Family – "Bella, Molly, & Scout", Ruby & Opal, and godmother Rachel

... psst, did you notice all of Piggie's favorite things hidden throughout the book? See if you can spot them all!